work that God sees

prayerful motherhood
in the midst of the overwhelm

---
seen
---

shannon guerra

Copyright © 2020 Shannon Guerra

All rights reserved. No part of this book may be reproduced in any form or by any electronic or mechanical means, including information storage and retrieval systems, without permission in writing from the publisher, except by reviewers, who may quote brief passages in a review.

ISBN 978-1-7345978-4-4
ISBN (ebook) 978-1-7345978-5-1

Scripture quotations are from the ESV® Bible (The Holy Bible, English Standard Version®), copyright © 2001 by Crossway, a publishing ministry of Good News Publishers. Used by permission. All rights reserved.

Portions of scripture in **bold** are the author's emphasis.

Cover design by Copperlight Wood

This title may be purchased in bulk for ministry or group study use. For more information, please email shop@copperlightwood.com.

Printed and bound in the United States of America

Published by Copperlight Wood
P.O. Box 870697
Wasilla, AK   99687

www.copperlightwood.com

for Jenna,

whose Father knows where she's going,

and loves watching her get there

Also by Shannon Guerra

Upside Down:
Understanding and Supporting Attachment in Adoptive and Foster Families

Oh My Soul:
Encountering God in Honest, Unconventional (and Sometimes Messy) Prayer

Oh My Soul Companion Journal

Oh My Soul Devotional:
21-Day Complete Study
3-Day Mini Studies

the Work That God Sees series:
Prayerful Motherhood in the Midst of the Overwhelm
Capable
Allied
Growing
Steadfast
Resilient
Seen

seen:
a definition
7

work that God sees
9

patience with joy:
cleaning house with Colossians
13

captain's log:
every day is an adventure
17

no boys allowed:
confessions from the unmentionables department
18

finding our focus
when we're hungry for answers
21

prayer:
the most rustic & dignified thing we can do
25

a little q & a:
learning to take God at His word
26

communion with Him:
how He moves us to the next chapter
31

in the fog:
what we do when we can't see where we're going
33

stronghold:
a safe place for those who know His name
38

the day of small things
39

how God sees us
43

clam chowder
the right way, and the other right way
44

questions
for personal journaling or group discussion
47

notes
50

seen

seen:
adjective. recognized, known

see also:
anticipated, attended to, contemplated,
gazed upon, esteemed, familiar,
identified, understood, watched over

held with regard

this is who you are.

work that God sees

Daylight increased rapidly, slanting into our house in ways we hadn't seen in a year. For example, I could see it reflecting off two pieces of old scotch tape on the ceiling, which must've been from the paper snowflakes that we hang at Christmastime every year. Except the previous year I had been sick and we kept everything on minimalist survival mode. Now that I thought of it, we didn't hang snowflakes that year.

So those pieces of tape were there for at least fifteen months and I never noticed.

And I left them on ceiling. Acknowledging their existence was an entirely different thing from taking the time to drag the piano bench over, stand on my tiptoes, and flail at small pieces of plastic that may or may not come off in one piece. The days were so full, just getting through the school day was enough to drive me batty.

Check this journal assignment. Print out these papers. Figure out how to multiply algebraic fractions. Find a map of Cape Horn. Check the progress of the avocado plant, and research exactly how toxic it is to cats. Specifically, black cats. More specifically, black kittens named Knightley who like to eat houseplants.

I didn't mind doing school with the kids. You might think I'm nuts for saying this, but I even kind of liked re-learning algebra with our oldest. It was a game, a puzzle, a mystery with a perfect solution. Give me a quiet room and some time with a sheet of paper and a sharp pencil, and I'm a happy, geeky camper.

What I *did* mind was trying to help one kid with algebra on my left while helping another kid with arithmetic on my right and fielding questions from two other kids in the room, all while keeping a covert eye on another child who preferred to do the potty dance rather than ask politely to go to the bathroom.

It was whiplash where I needed white space, and it made me the grumpiest camper in the house.

I noticed that I was getting super peevish when they repeatedly asked the same question, taking turns in five minute increments. I hated answering the same thing over and over and over.

What's for dinner? When's Dad coming home? Are you going to share that chocolate?

My answers (and temper) got pretty short. *Food. Later. Are you kidding?!*

Another sore point was interruptions, which I thought we had conquered, but these things crop up again after a while like Bad Manners Whack-A-Mole. It fried me in no time at all when I was in the middle of an important talk with one kid only to have another kiddo (or two or three) come in and simultaneously ask, argue, or complain about something as urgent as who left the jar of peanut butter on the counter.

Before I boiled over, I sent two-thirds of them outside — all the math I had brainpower left for — and gutted a squash for dinner. *Are they ever listening? Don't they see what I'm already doing?*

The honest answer was No, not always. And part of it, I knew, was that I needed to be listening closer and seeing them more, too. So much of it comes back to the mama and the environment created by her own attitude.

But another part of it was that they should not have to hear or see everything, because we are not doing our work for bragging rights, recognition, or applause. We are doing a work that God sees.

> *And why they went I cannot tell: some say it was to win gold. It may be so; but the noblest deeds which have been done on earth have not been done for gold. It was not for the sake of gold that the Lord came down and died, and the Apostles went out to preach the good news in all lands...*
>
> *And there are heroes in our days also, who do noble deeds, but not for gold. Our discoverers did not go to make themselves rich when they sailed out one after another in to the dreary frozen seas, nor did the ladies who went out last year to drudge in the hospitals of the East, making themselves poor, that they might be rich in noble works. And young men, too, whom you know, children, and some of them of your own kin, did they say to themselves, "How much money shall I earn?" when they went out to the war, leaving wealth, and comfort, and a pleasant home, and all that money can give, to face hunger and thirst, and wounds and death, that they might fight for their country and their Queen? No, children, there is a better thing on earth than wealth, a better thing than life itself, and that is, to have done something before you die, for which good men may honour you, and God your Father smile upon your work.*
>
> *– Charles Kingsley* [1]

Yes. All of that. But still, it would be nice to know something grand is coming out of all of this mundane chaos. The laundry will always need to be done, the budget will always need to be met, and the lessons (academic and otherwise) will always need to be taught. Tomorrow, we'll wake up and do it all over again, and our kids will be one day older. And so will we. And where are we going with all of these days, anyway?

Is it someplace grand? Is it something beyond dishes and manners and algebra?

And He answers in scripture, in His own words:

Truly, truly, I say to you, whoever believes in me will also do the works that I do; and greater works than these will he do, because I am going to the Father.

– John 14:12

At first, honestly, I didn't think this was a very helpful answer because I've never understood it. We will do greater things than He did? I checked the Greek, and "greater" really does mean *greater*: larger, older, louder, more.

Greater things than this we will do...did You really mean that? Is that what we're doing? How is that possible?

Yes, I meant that, He said, *and it's possible for many reasons. But for starters...well, Love, I was never a mother.*

patience with joy
cleaning house with Colossians

That morning, our kitchen counter held a pile of apple cores, scattered books and pencils, a sheet of stickers, a ribbon, a closed laptop, and a phone drying out in a baggie of rice. Crowding the edge by the sink were several dirty dishes and a warped-but-drying weekly planner, salvaged from a coffee spill that stained it through December…in case you were wondering why the phone was drying out in the first place.

Not every day was this messy. Some days were far worse.

I kept trying to clean it throughout the day. I put the dishes in the dishwasher, turned back around, and four art projects magically took their place. I gathered up pencils and books, put them away, and came back to find an abacus, a bottle of glue, and a stack of construction paper. It was like trying to slay the hydra.

I knew these days were brief — a blink, a flick of a page. Random strangers I met in public told me so quite often, right after taking a head count of the kids and saying, "My, your hands are full."

> *And so, from the day we heard, we have not ceased to pray for you, asking that you may be*

filled with the knowledge of his will in all spiritual wisdom and understanding, so as to walk in a manner worthy of the Lord, fully pleasing to him, bearing fruit in every good work and increasing in the knowledge of God.

– Colossians 1:9-10

Our baby was in kindergarten, and as she practiced her handwriting I heard myself saying things like, *Go slow, carefully, and you'll only have to do it once. You won't need the eraser.*

The kittens, those tiny twerpedoes, still could not be trusted when we left the house, so we locked them in my bedroom. When I was running late, the act of trying to contain them both perfectly demonstrated the chaos implied in the phrase "herding kittens." I couldn't even get out the door before at least one of them flew past me, escaping toward the stairs.

And I heard God telling me, too: *Go slow, carefully, and you'll only have to do it once.*

May you be strengthened with all power, *according to his glorious might,* ***for all endurance and patience with joy,*** *giving thanks to the Father, who has qualified you to share in the inheritance of the saints in light.*

– Colossians 1:11-12

It was when I was finishing a post the night before that I spilled the coffee – moving too fast, too late at night, too much on my mind, and the decaf went flying. It splashed all over the calendar, the schedule, the to-do lists, the whole mess. It was a fitting end to a day that felt stained and darkened. I shook off the planner and scrubbed the floor while the pages soaked it all in.

> *He has delivered us from the domain of darkness and transferred us to the kingdom of his beloved Son, in whom we have redemption, the forgiveness of sins.*
>
> *– Colossians 1:13-14*

And He was teaching me to soak it in, too – to notice more, to pray more, to enjoy more. *Be bold, Love, but with care and caution,* He said. *You won't need the eraser.*

A clean house is good for everyone who lives and visits there. But tidiness starts within us.

> *Put to death therefore what is earthly in you: sexual immorality, impurity, passion, evil desire, and covetousness, which is idolatry…But now you must put them all away: anger, wrath, malice, slander, and obscene talk from your mouth.*
>
> *Do not lie to one another, seeing that you have put off the old self with its practices and have put on the new self, which is being renewed in knowledge after the image of its creator.*
>
> *Put on then, as God's chosen ones, holy and beloved, compassionate hearts, kindness, humility, meekness, and patience, bearing with one another and, if one has a complaint against another, forgiving each other; as the Lord has forgiven you, so you also must forgive. And above all these put on love, which binds everything together in perfect harmony.*

And let the peace of Christ rule in your hearts, to which indeed you were called in one body. And be thankful.

- Colossians 3:5, 8-10, 12-15

The stains on the days in my planner lessened as the weeks passed. Every week was the flick of a new page, with less stain, more sanctification.

You know what, Love? God asked me. *Maybe everything on your to-do list isn't so crucial. Maybe it doesn't all have to get done today because the pressure of doing is harassment from the enemy to keep you from peace and simplicity, too distracted from the important things.*

Maybe we just need to love these kids, and enjoy our coffee. Drink some water. Take deep breaths. Pray bold prayers. God will throw the windows open to allow fresh air in as soon as we ask Him to.

Captain's Log, day 5473:

Whoever said, "There are no stupid questions" never had their fourteen-year-old ask,
"Hey Mom - when can we get a gong?"

These days are filled with exciting moments, such as a child flushing underwear down the potty, and my discovery that Knightley has been using my toothbrush.

Tonight I'm pleased to report that all underwear is accounted for, and I have a new toothbrush.

Also, our kittens are plaque-free.

no boys allowed
confessions from the unmentionables department

Just slip quietly into the aisle, make a quick turn behind a clothing rack, and stay cool.

The furtive glances. The reckless rifling through racks of clothing. The frantic search for just the right size, and fighting panic at the sudden sound of a man's voice as he's walking down the tile path, twenty feet away.

I'm not shoplifting, I promise. It's worse than that. I'm...I'm...buying unmentionables. Somebody get me out of here.

I'm completely rational about a host of other things. I actually enjoy the dentist; I don't mind getting my teeth cleaned. Mondays don't bother me at all. But there's almost nothing I dread more than shopping for underwear.

One rack over, another woman is across from me and we carefully avoid eye contact. I rummage through satins and polyesters (egad), scanning tags for the perfect size, just to be met with a gibbering combination of letters and numbers that only mean something to adorable highschoolers who have never experienced childbirth.

I hear a male voice nearby, and the praise I whisper for being barely five feet tall and hidden by the rack of hosiery is immediately followed by the sudden desire to curse the young woman who brought her boyfriend in.

I think I prayed instead, but can't be certain. It was all so distressing.

34C. 36B. 42A, and on and on. French-cut, high-cut, bikini-cut, and brief. *I'm going to need counseling after this.*

There ought to be a precise algorithm just for women who have been through childbirth and breastfeeding to assist us in finding the perfect fit and style of undergarment. It would go something like this:

> *Start with the size you were before your first pregnancy. Add x for every childbirth, multiply by y for every child breastfed, divide by the number of actual months nursing. Finally, subtract n times pi for how many years it's been since weaning your youngest child, and proceed to the nearest liquor store.*

Lacking this perfect formula (and not being in the habit of frequenting liquor stores anyway), I skeptically grab a few items that look like they might fit a female human, and then contemplate my dash to the dressing room...and suddenly realize that I don't remember where the dressing room is.

Blankety blank. I should've checked before my arms were loaded with lacy unmentionables.

From between a rack of hideous negligees and cute pajama pants, I peek out and look for the sign. Ah, there it is, just to the right. *Awesome. Yes! Except...oh, wait...*

Under the sign, between me and the dressing room, is the Designated Waiting Area for Patient Husbands. And two men are sitting there.

Oh, expletive.

I grab several more things off the rack next to me – every possible style in four different sizes, doesn't matter what, as long as the pile of garments is high enough to obscure my face. In our smallish town, this is the last place I want to be recognized from school, from work, or, God forbid, from church. I double-time it past them and duck into the hallway.

I survive the dressing room. A few things make the cut, I make the purchase, and then make haste to the car.

The herbal relaxant I took earlier was probably an excellent idea. Shopping online would have been a better one, though.

finding our focus
when we're hungry for answers

The sunlight melted the snow to into nothing, blinding you if you looked at it. I knew winter wasn't over yet because we often get snow in May, but you could feel spring coming. There was no stopping it.

French bread dough sat on the counter, rising in a sunbeam. I had intended to make two loaves, but instead kept cutting off chunks of it to fry in butter like naan, but far more rustic; I didn't even roll it out like a civilized person. I stretched it out with my hands, all quick-and-dirty like, as the butter melted in the pan. If you ever try this as your flatbread for a grilled BLT, you'll thank me later.

There was no time for the bread to rise because I was frantic and hungry, stealing a hasty break between school and playtime and bickering and chores. I flung out aggravated prayers while I flipped the bread, asking God to show a certain child more of Him. Asking Him to make my child look at Him, see Him, and pay attention. All those things I'd been trying to tell that kid for the past week, month, year.

And God said, *No*.

What? I watched the bread turn up at the edges, heard the butter sizzle against it. What do You mean, No?

He said, *You look at Me more, Love. They will notice.*

Just like when you see people stopped along the road, watching something, and you look, too. Just like you how you tell them to mind their own business and stop bossing and tattling on each other — you just focus on your own vision. Look more at Me, toward Me, and they will shift their direction, too.

The sunlight slanted in and things looked different just from the new light cast on it. Sure, it showed streaks and water spots on the windows, but the light shined on both sides, and what was bleak suddenly had color.

We walk in fear when all we see is shadows and darkness. Prognoses that we thought were grim are strangely hopeful when a wise person speaks into them. I had just read about this as I chugged through 2 Samuel:

Now there was a famine in the days of David for three years, year after year. And David sought the face of the Lord.

- *2 Samuel 21:1a*

Three years is a long time to be hungry. Had David been asking all that time, and he finally heard after three years? Or did he search for an answer on his own in all the ways he could think for three years before finally asking?

I've been on both sides, myself.

Our perspectives are greatly influenced by the news we're reading, the people we listen to, and the thoughts we allow to run rampant in our head. The margin we build into the edges of our days changes depending on our focus, shrinking or widening in proportion to the fear and anxiety we allow into our hearts. Sometimes I ask Him right away, other times I'm frantic and run to Google or a friend first, forgetting that the One with the answer is right here, close as breath.

I was frantic and hungry, and the margin that ought to be rising like bread dough was being rapidly consumed instead — and He still tells me the answer is so simple.

Look at Me, Love.

For you are my lamp, O Lord, and my God lightens my darkness.

- 2 Samuel 22:29

I hungered for answers about the darkness and shadows some of our kiddos came from. The research was daunting, though: fetal alcohol syndrome, neglect and trauma, what is damaged, what can be repaired, and what professionals agree about being beyond hope.

Maybe in your family it's something else – a different diagnosis, a looming debt, a relational deficit. God has the final say, regardless of dark predictions and bleak prognoses. Redemption is everywhere. He made us to be redeemed, to take thoughts captive. He made us to renew our mind. He made us to be more than conquerors, image bearers of the King.

He made us to look like Him, to know His face, to show His face to others.

For by you I can run against a troop, and by my God I can leap over a wall.

- 2 Samuel 22:30

Our eyes are on Him, not the waves around us. Not the propaganda on the news, not the negativity on social media, not the squabbling of children. We address what must not be neglected, but we are consumed by His goodness and truth. We hold our questions, fears, and assumptions up to Him, and let go – dropping them on the altar to see what Truth says about it. What is left, surviving His crucible, is true.

> *This God—his way is perfect; the word of the Lord proves true; he is a shield for all those who take refuge in him.*
>
> *- 2 Samuel 22:31*

He heals. He saves. He turns all things for good. And He's doing it right now, even in those shadows where we can't see. Look, see, pay attention: He is making all things new, and His light is overtaking the darkness. There's no stopping it. And when we focus on that, our kids can't help noticing it, too.

Prayer is extreme.
It is at once the most rustic thing we can do and the most dignified thing we can do; it is both the humblest and most audacious move simultaneously.
We need God. And we can approach Him, the Creator of all things, knowing that He not only hears us, but that He also wants to.

a little of & a
learning to take God at His word

If you spend any time at all with someone between the ages of three to ten, you're probably an expert at both answering and deferring questions ranging anywhere from bungee jumping to bug poop. Like so:

"Mom," Chamberlain asked, "are you going to be a goop or a dainty lady when you're a grandma?"

"Umm..." I stalled, accidentally slamming the rack of dishes in the dishwasher.

Cham squinted, resigning herself to the truth. "Probably a goop."

Or this:

"Why are they always called *mailmen* and *firemen*?" she asked. "Because girls can be them, too."

"Because sometimes 'man' just means human." I told her. "It can mean men or women. We don't have to be fussy about it."

"Oh. Because *firehuman* would sound weird." Yep, it would.

Those are easy ones. But there's also this:

"Do you think you have enough chocolate to eat if you have another baby?"

For reals. To which, after spitting out my coffee, I answered something like, "No – I mean, I don't know –

I mean, it's none of your business. *Sheesh*." A whole six months had passed since her brother was born, and most of my days were consumed with wrestling his slick alligator-roll moves, quadrupling the time it took to change diapers and get him dressed.

But if you spend time with kids older than ten, the questions are different – sometimes they're way harder emotionally, sometimes they're rhetorical, and sometimes they go both ways. Like so:

"Mom, can I (fill-in-the-blank) yet?"

And often my answer is something like, "I dunno, did you (apologize to your brother/do your chores/fill-in-another-blank) yet?"

Sometimes the exchange runs like this:

"Yes, I have."

"No, you haven't."

"Yes, I have, because…"

"No, you haven't, because…" You know how this goes. The ping-pong of accountability balanced with love is exhausting.

And sometimes afterwards it sounds like:

"I love you."

"Well, you don't act like it. If you loved me, you'd let me (fill-in-the-blank)."

And, oh Jesus, let my words be few. People need love the most when they act the most unloving, and sometimes kids can prove it until we're drained sapless and need some pretty serious love ourselves. At the end of these days I am praying deep and wide, brief and long, in spurts and spasms, whatever it takes to redeem the mess of misbehavior and consequences and rebellion and flat-out lying the previous twelve hours held.

I'm in the Word and looking for answers, and my bookmark in the Old Testament is in Ecclesiastes.

But then I looked at everything under the sun, and saw that it was useless to read Ecclesiastes while discouraged, exhausted, and PMSing. *This, too, is a grievous task and striving after the wind.*

So I moved to Psalm 147 instead and bent into it, head in hands, elbows on a gritty countertop, surrounded by a rice cooker, a crockpot, and a couple of dirty dishcloths. Like so:

He heals the brokenhearted and binds up their wounds. Verse three.

Great is our Lord and mighty in power; His understanding has no limit. Verse five.

And I know this. You know this. But we can be pretty hard on ourselves, and some days (or some years) we are a long ways away from feeling the truth of it. And we think, *If it were true, it would feel true…wouldn't it?*

I keep reading.

The LORD delights in those who fear him, who put their hope in his unfailing love. Verse eleven.

I stop here. *You take delight in me? Really? Because it doesn't feel like it. We were really roughing it today (this week, this year) and I'm not sure "delight" was anywhere to be found here.*

And I realize I sound just like the kid who smarted off to me earlier when I said "I love you." *Well, you don't act like it. If you loved me, You'd fix this. If You delighted in me, you'd heal this. You'd let me (fill-in-the-blank).*

But, like my kid, I'm basing my grievance of the moment on feelings – those changeable, flighty things – instead of unfailing, fixed truth. My feelings are not only manipulating me, but also trying to manipulate God the same way my kids try manipulate me every once in a while. And feelings…well, they're harder to wrestle down than a squirmy six-month-old during a diaper change.

I switch to the New Testament and my bookmark is in the beginning of Luke. Right out of the gate people are told the impossible, and it happens more than once:

The barren conceive and have a son, the virgin conceives and has the Savior. Did they *feel* like they could have children? No, and no. But the truth is right here, and it continues to make history:

For nothing will be impossible for God.

– Luke 1:37

And the Lord starts giving me some answers.

Hey, Love...you, who feel stuck. You, who feel like you've been speaking to a wall and getting nowhere. You, tired of waiting, and wondering if it's all for nothing and time to give up and lower your hopes and expectations. Let Me tell you something.

Praying works. Worship works. Even when it doesn't look like it, they work. But there's something else you need to know.

Acknowledging My presence also works.

Truth is quietly confident while our feelings are often impetuous, knocking into things with sudden enthusiasm. And the truth is that God is a better parent than I am. So if I have my kid's best in mind while I fumble through this parenting thing, I can trust that He has my best in mind while He has the entire universe at His holy fingertips.

And blessed is she who believed that there would be a fulfillment of what was spoken to her from the Lord.

– Luke 1:45

We are so often tempted to water down what we believe based on temporary circumstances, as though His truth were limited to that. But what if we took Him at His word? What if He has promised something amazing – and He has – and we believed Him in spite of our circumstances?

There's nothing the enemy could do to thwart it. There's nothing you or I could do to change it.

And His mercy is for those who fear Him from generation to generation.

– Luke 1:50

We ask Him our questions, and He quietly answers with His own: *Do you believe Me, Love? Will you trust Me?*

Because when you are out of words and out of ideas and out of temper, the act of recognizing that I am right there with you works. So many people pray out of habit or desperation and don't even think that there's a real Listener, fully God and fully Man, right there next to them. But I'm right there. And the harder habit of continually recognizing my presence in all the moments of your day – when you are pouring your coffee, when you are tempted to yell at your kids, when you are scrolling through Facebook and procrastinating about the laundry all over the couch – when you recognize that I am right there with you, it works.

Your prayer is more effective. Your worship is more powerful. And then I can give you all the words and ideas and answers you need, because when you acknowledge Me, you are also a listener.

God's not annoyed by our questions any more than He is intimidated by our posturing. He delights in those who know they can trust Him, steady on, in spite of what feels impossible.

communion with him
how He moves us to the next chapter

We took communion today. I don't know how your church does it, or if you even go to church, but at ours it's always on the first Sunday of the month and it usually catches me by surprise – like, Oh, it's a new month already. And for a second I feel like I'm behind or must've missed something, but I didn't; it's just that I'm remembering again that we're doing a new thing. Now we're doing May, not April.

A kid broke my heart today in a brand-new way, but an hour later he apologized for something he did yesterday that I'd already forgotten about. This parenting gig is full of whiplash and surprises.

I was thinking on it while holding that cracker and the tiny cup of juice:

The bread, the Body that says, *I paid for this* – the disobedience, the disrespect, the failures and depression and lack and all the things we can't do over.

And the juice, the Blood that says, *I'm doing a new thing, Love, do you not perceive it?* – the healing, the forgiveness, the reparation, the leaves budding in new growth, life flowing through things that looked dead and without hope.

I'm reading Mark 15 where He gives us the Body and the Blood, and if you don't know the end of the story it's a pretty bleak chapter. Here are the subheadings in my Bible:

Jesus delivered to Pilate
Pilate delivers Jesus to be crucified
Jesus is mocked
The Crucifixion
The death of Jesus
Jesus is buried

And it looks like the story is over.

Our lives carry similar subheadings in different seasons. They might look like this:

Major diagnosis
Best friend moves away
Pet dies
Child is sick
Laid off work
Can't pay bills
Divorce or death

And it looks like the story is over.

But it's not. The next chapter is Mark 16, and it starts with this subheading:

The Resurrection

And that's coming in our story, too. It's not over yet. And we haven't missed it; we're not behind.

We are human and imperfect and in need of communion with Him – and every time, He grabs me like someone who fell down and needs help getting up – because I do – and He says, *Hey Love, stop looking back there. We're doing a new thing.*

in the fog
what we do
when we can't see where we're going

Baby napping. Toddler playing sweetly, but loud enough to trigger neighborhood car alarms. Vin and I bossing him. Baby waking up after a refreshing 90-second power nap. Repeat until dinnertime.

And this, at least, has not changed in eighteen years of parenting – only then, it was two different kids who are both now in high school, and we are now old…er.

It is a good night for an easy dinner after a hard day of cringing from loud noises and not getting nearly enough done. Leftover pasta, leftover salad; sauté some broccoli to go over the top and give myself something to be proud of. Because some days feel like nothing to be proud of.

Not enough time for everyone and everything. Heaviness in the chest. A sense of swelling behind the eyes that hints at tears, but no thank you, we don't want that, we don't have time for that. In this season, ain't nobody got time for that.

I know what it is. It feels a little like PMS but it isn't – it's spiritual attack threatening to spiral into depression, the barrage of lies that shout *failure* from the rooftops in every area. The noise on the outside spikes against the noise inside. The body hurts, the mind and spirit hurt.

And I can be a slow learner, but now I know the drill when it hits: Do the small things, the necessary things that fight the negative thoughts and the feelings and the oversensitive body processes.

Drink a glass of water. Take a dose of vitamin D. Rebuke the lies.

And find something easy to clean.

People sometimes are surprised at how relatively clean our house is in spite of seven kids living here, and usually the credit goes to regular chores and a highly efficient husband. But every once in a while, it's something else entirely.

Every once in a while, the house is clean because *the mama almost lost her ever-loving mind, but made a narrow escaped by taking it out on the kitchen.* Because order on the outside helps bring order to the inside. And wiping down counters is easy, so much easier than the stressful intangibles that have no end. Clean counters help bring sanity and white space.

I cannot clean everything. Just like I cannot do everything. But I can clean this counter in front of me, and see the difference. In so many areas, we can believe and hope and trust that what we do matters, but we cannot see it yet and the enemy takes advantage of that.

So doing something that we can see is important. It becomes prayer and prophecy; we see movement and change and impact. A clean counter can represent so much more as we pray.

The edge of the sink is covered in coffee grounds and water droplets. One wipe, and it's clean. Perfect. Rinse the sponge. Done.

There's a clear before-and-after here, unlike most of the other work with words, situations, and people. And my own attitude.

For many of us, this is a season of refining, pressing further than we thought we could go, pushing through pain, taking maturity to the next level. And it hurts, like a muscle being strengthened.

We are refining character and relationships, habits, skills, and communication, working toward a great plan that we cannot fully see, praying for rain but not yet seeing the cloud the size of a hand.[2]

He sees what we cannot see – and sometimes, often, He lets us see these things for each other.

A close friend of ours had a surprise party for her fortieth birthday. She was blindfolded; she didn't know where she was going or when she would arrive. But her friends knew, and we couldn't wait for her to get there.

> *...As Christians, we will always live in tension between what we understand and what remains a mystery....We cannot afford to live only in what we understand because then we don't grow or progress anymore; we just travel the same familiar roads we have traveled all of our Christian life. It is important that we expose ourselves to impossibilities that force us to have questions that we cannot answer.*
>
> *– Bill Johnson* [3]

In the deep searching, when we trust God because it feels like we have no choice but to trust Him (and is that really trust at all?) we're pressed into voicing those gut-honest questions – the ones He's not afraid of, but that we're usually afraid to ask.

These questions lay us open, vulnerable to legalistic blind spots in our past, and the enemy hisses things like, *If you really trusted God, you wouldn't feel that way, or need to ask that question, or feel so uncertain.* We think that Really Good Christians are supposed to find some kind of bliss in the pressure of not knowing, but that's only because the enemy is liar.

The crucible is for silver, and the furnace is for gold, and the Lord tests hearts.

– Proverbs 17:3

God knows these seasons are not easy for us. He's not mad at us for feeling the fire and asking the hard questions.

He's not mad at us when we ask repeatedly for the cloud the size of a hand.

He's right there with the truth – He knows the destination, and these questions are the sweet spot, the brave willingness to stare fears in the face and name them aloud, willing to surrender those fears to Him.

Here's the root of it: If it really is that bad and our fears come to pass, will we still trust Him? Will we still talk to Him?

Of course we will. There is no one left. He is the only one who knows how to take us where we're supposed to be going.

Regardless of what the weather or the circumstances look like, He is leaning forward, rubbing His hands in anticipation, telling us, *Just wait, you're going to love this. I can't wait to show you where you're going.*

Those who fear You shall see me and rejoice, because I have hoped in Your word.

– Psalm 119:74

These curveballs, these situations of unknowing and what-in-the-world-are-You-doing, prove to us that surrender is beautiful, powerful, and victorious, and that He knows what we want better than we do. He's not afraid to give it to us, even when we're afraid to ask for it or to take it.

The unknowing and waiting are a lot like writing. Here too, we usually do not know where we are going:

> *At its best, the sensation of writing is that of any unmerited grace. It is handed to you, but only if you look for it. You search, you break your heart, your back, your brain, and then – and only then – it is handed to you. From the corner of your eye you see motion. Something is moving through the air and headed your way.*
>
> *….You find and finger a phrase at a time; you lay it down cautiously, as if with tongs, and wait suspended until the next one finds you: Ah yes, then this; and yes, praise be, then this.*
>
> *– Annie Dillard* [4]

Bread crumbs from lunch cover the island. I scoop them into my hand, throw them off the deck for the birds, or maybe the mice, but with four cats I'm not worried. Easy, done. Moving on.

It's hard to see outside of ourselves when the stress and chaos press in, closing in on us just like the fog around the windows, obscuring mountains, neighbors, and the river of traffic going up and down the highway.

We ask for a cloud the size of a hand, and in perfect time He sends the fog rolling in, pressing us into questions and answers and growth we could not or would not have pursued otherwise. And sometimes in our own density, we don't recognize that that, too, is an answer.

> The Lord is a stronghold for the oppressed,
> a stronghold in times of trouble.
> And those who know your name put their
> trust in you, for you, O Lord,
> have not forsaken those who seek you.
> - Psalm 9:9-10

Stronghold: a fortified place protecting those within it from attack.

So, shhh...you can rest.
The gates are locked,
and the Stronghold guards
your family, your sleep,
and the days ahead.

the day of small things

He was our smallest baby, but by that winter when he turned fifteen, our oldest kid wore Vince's shirts that had shrunk in the wash. He could reach things off the high shelves in the kitchen, open tight jars for me, and chop wood. He even (gasp) shaved.

On his big day, he went with Vince and four of his siblings on a birthday outing while I stayed home with the other two kids, in charge of making birthday lunch. He requested homemade clam chowder. Piece of cake.

I chopped potatoes and onions, and kept an eye on the two boys who spun gears in the dining room, wearing the varnish off the table. Maybe I should've stopped them. Maybe I should've told them to simmer down, just a little. But I didn't – it was a beautiful moment, them playing together like normal kids, making noise and messes and laughing memories. We needed more of this.

The music was loud and the sun streamed in, and the house was completely still aside from the shrieking activity around the table and the flames under the soup pot. Maybe that doesn't describe stillness to you, but to me it was like our house was in a coma.

*What to do, what to do...*once the soup was simmering, I was at a loss. It's astonishing how inspired you can be with three shots of espresso and only two kids in the house.

I could read. I could open the laptop and work on that file of 60,000 words. I could wash the kitchen windows. I could re-pot the rootbound plant on the counter. I could do almost anything short of flying to the moon — but no, I only had a few minutes before everyone came back home, and I had to keep an eye on the stove to keep what was simmering from scorching.

So I scrubbed the grime and grungus off the sink stopper. Such a little thing. So insignificant.

The hot water ran and the steam rose, and stainless steel started to shine again. The sun hit it and sparkled, and I realized this was the first day of blue skies after a week of dreary, smeary grey in the weary early winter.

> *We had our first frost last night – this morning the lawns are all grey, with a pale, bright sunshine on them: wonderfully beautiful. And somehow exciting. The first beginning of winter always excites me; it makes me want adventures.*
>
> – C. S. Lewis [5]

The big boy and crew came back hungry for chowder and full of news about the new Lego store. That kid got his first Lego set when he was three years old. That was only ten minutes ago, and suddenly he was building them into robots. Little things into big things.

> *...but who dare despise the day of small things, if it has proved to be the dawn of mighty ones?*

– Charles Kingsley [6]

It was like the granny square afghan I'd been working on for years (you could tell how long I'd been working on it, because the orange-brown-green color scheme dated it back to the sixties…kidding, but not kidding) and it was finally down to just two squares and trimming left. In these days of imported department store specials, it felt both trivial and sacred to spend time on it compared to everything else going on in and around us. There's always more to be learned, taught, cooked, cleaned, hugged, organized, and disciplined; the dishes and laundry are never done. There are pages to read, and pages to write.

And there is always more stitching to do. But, you've heard me say this before: the difference with stitching is that you can see exactly what progress has been made.

A finished book can go on a shelf, but there's no way to measure what was really absorbed in the reading. The laundry hamper will be full again tomorrow. And you can teach and lecture and assign consequences till the cows come home, but those kids are still going to tie fake spiders to the tail of their little brother's favorite stuffed animal, and try to make the cat walk on his front legs wheelbarrow style, and color their own body parts with a green marker. I've, um, heard it happens. In some families.

But with that blanket, I could see exactly what was accomplished. This row, that round of colors, done. And that is incredibly satisfying in the midst of all the other intangibles.

That fifteen-year-old boy is now an adult living on his own, and the blanket belongs to him. But thanks to two surprise pregnancies, we are still in the same place we were then: Our kids are big and little, busy and slow, high school and infant, and life is full of their needs and their changes and their noise.

These days I still sometimes feel rootbound, spinning gears. I still type one-handed, holding another little boy who will be a big fifteen-year-old in about ten minutes. There are a million things I could do, but I don't regret holding him. I don't regret keeping an eye on these kids to keep what is simmering in them from scorching.

The dirty socks, the worn-down pencils, the wet diapers. The never-ending housework and teaching and cooking. All these minutes that fill long and short days – these are the small things, baby steps, that lead to mighty movements. God sees every one of them, and it is the sacred monotony of faithfulness in these early days that write history.

He looks at us the way we look
at our kids when we are in the best
state of mothering -
in the deepest love for our children,
when we look at our sleeping babies
and just want
to kiss their faces off.

That's how He looks at us every time:
Supremely satisfied with us as we
are, not because we don't need to
grow or change (we do, just like our
kids) but because He sees us
as He intends us to be.

He sees you purely, without any
filters of fault, imperfection, or
as-yet-unmet potential.

He sees you perfectly.

clam chowder
the right way, and the other right way

I grew up thinking there was only one way to eat clam chowder. We didn't even call it "New England style" – though you can bet that in our pre-cooking days, we made sure that's what the label on the can said – because nobody ate the other kind. Manhattan clam chowder? *Tomatoes* in clam chowder, ugh, are you kidding me? It wasn't even an option. It was the Wrong Way.

Until two of our kids couldn't have dairy, at least, and then I tried it. And I learned (as I have with many things) that I was wrong – Manhattan style is amazing. It's the Other Right Way to make clam chowder.

So here are both ways to do it.

Main ingredients for either version:
2-3 cans (6.5 oz size) of minced or chopped clams
1 onion, chopped
4 large potatoes, diced
4-8 cooked strips of bacon, chopped into small bits

Now, here our roads diverge. If you've read *Capable*, you'll notice that New England style is just a variation of that dairy-loving potato chowder. So let's do that first:

For New England style, you also need:

6(ish) cups of milk. Or, you can use a cup or two of cream, and make up the difference with broth. Just don't use water, because you love yourself.

¼ to ½ cup each of flour AND butter. But they must be equal amounts. More flour and butter equals a thicker chowder.

1 t. Worcestershire sauce. Or substitute with red wine, which is much easier to pronounce (unless you drank the rest of the bottle, in which case you might not be able to pronounce anything, and probably should've stuck with the Worcestershire sauce).

Directions:

1. Sauté the onion in the butter on low for a few minutes.

2. Add the chopped potatoes and stir to mix with the onions, roughly coating everything with butter.

3. Do the roux! Sprinkle the flour over the potatoes and onions, and STIR STIR STIR again to coat everything with flour, which should be mostly absorbed by the butter. Immediately add 1 cup of milk and stir as it starts to thicken.

4. Continue adding milk (or cream, or broth) a cup at a time as it heats and thickens, and keep stirring. Turn the heat to low so the potatoes can soften without scorching.

5. While you are stirring and adding the milk/cream/broth, add the chopped bacon and Worcestershire sauce.

And, if it helps, in our house it's called WURST-uh-SHUR. I'm here for you.

6. Ready for clams? Not so fast! Open the cans and add only the liquid. If you add the clams now, they will turn to rubber. RESIST, I tell you.

7. Once the potatoes are tender, add the clams. Also add salt/pepper to taste.

Easy, right? No? Well, just wait until you try...

Manhattan style, which also needs:
2 stalks of celery, chopped
1 carrot, chopped
1 16-oz can of crushed or diced tomatoes
2-3 cups of broth
1 T. butter
1 t. thyme

Directions:

1. Saute the onion, carrots, and celery in the butter for a few minutes.

2. Add potatoes, tomatoes (liquid and all), broth, and thyme. Simmer on low.

3. When the veggies are tender, add the clams, including the liquid. Season with salt and pepper, and...DONE.

See? I told you this was the other right way to do it.

questions
for personal journaling or group discussion

work that God sees:

What work has God watched me do today?

What work have I seen God do today?

What small thing can I change to help me pay better attention to my kids?

patience with joy:

What beautiful details are in this season – in our home, in our routines, in our relationships?

How can I slow down to enjoy these days more? What specific things can I do this week to facilitate more joy?

How can I put on compassion, kindness, humility, meekness, and patience today? What would that look like?

finding our focus:

When do my kids see me look at Jesus? How can I shift my gaze to Him more?

What kind of margin do I want to build into our days?

What questions, fears, or assumptions do I need to surrender to the Lord right now?

a little q & a:

What feelings have I had lately that need to be directed to truth? What true statements can I focus on when those feelings come?

What are some of the routines of my day when the Lord is right there with me?

What great things has God promised me, both in His written Word and in His words to me as I listen to Him?

in the fog:

What gut-honest questions have I been afraid to ask God about?

What gut-honest desires have I been afraid to ask for?

What growth has He pressed me into that I would not have pursued on my own? How has it made me more like Him?

the day of small things:

What examples of sacred monotony are filling my days? How can I see more beauty and encouragement in them?

What big and small projects do I look forward to working on whenever I get a chance? How can I pray toward those, while still living in gratitude for these small days?

What mighty things in my children's (and family's) future do I want to start praying toward – or, start praying about more often?

1. Charles Kingsley, *The Heroes* (1889), public domain – accessed reprint from BiblioBazaar, page 51.

2. See 1 Kings 18 – specifically, verse 44: *And at the seventh time he said, "Behold, a little cloud like a man's hand is rising from the sea." And he said, "Go up, say to Ahab, 'Prepare your chariot and go down, lest the rain stop you.'"*

3. Bill Johnson, *The Supernatural Power of a Transformed Mind* (Shippensburg, PA: Destiny Image Publishers, Inc., 2005), 75.

4. Annie Dillard, *The Writing Life* (New York: Harper Perennial, 1989), 75-76.

5. C.S. Lewis, *Letters to Children* (New York: Simon & Schuster, 1985), 56-57.

6. Charles Kingsley, *Westward Ho!*, 2 vols. (New York: J.F. Taylor and Company, 1899), 1:2.

Also by Shannon Guerra

"What makes this book stand out from other contemporary Christian writings on prayer is the author's crisp prose and sharp sense of humor... An insightful, honest, and genuinely funny author delivers a standout devotional."

- *Kirkus Reviews*

It's significant that paper is made from the same material He was nailed to. He still uses it to heal us, show us more of Him, and conquer what's harassing us.

Available wherever books are sold, and at **copperlightwood.com**

Adoptive and foster families often feel alone, but it doesn't have to be that way. Shannon Guerra learned this first-hand after she and her husband adopted two children in 2012, and she started writing shockingly transparent blog posts about what her family was going through at home, at the doctor's office, and in her heart as a mama.

And adoptive and foster families started writing back. Their overwhelming, unanimous theme was, "This is what I've wanted to tell people for so long. **I wish everyone who knows our family could read this.**"

Upside Down is the result. Because adoptive & foster families should never feel alone, & communities can be equipped to make sure they never feel that way again.

one more thing...

Do you want more encouragement in the season you're in? Do you want to grow deep and wide, regardless of your space and circumstances?

You are warmly invited to copperlightwood.com where we're transparent about finding peace in the hard moments, beauty in the mess, and white space in the chaos. It's a little unpolished here, so watch out for the Legos on the floor.

His peace is for you,

Shannon Guerra

subscribe:
eepurl.com/MugpP

connect:
instagram.com/copperlightwood
facebook.com/copperlightwood
goodreads.com/shannonguerra

www.ingramcontent.com/pod-product-compliance
Lightning Source LLC
Chambersburg PA
CBHW021133080526
44587CB00012B/1268